NOSE NINJAS!

By Tracy Vonder Brink

Clever Critters

TABLE OF CONTENTS

A Crabtree Seedlings Book

Crabtree Publishing

crabtreebooks.com

School-to-Home Support for Caregivers and Teachers

This book helps children grow by letting them practice reading. Here are a few guiding questions to help readers build comprehension skills. Possible answers appear here in red.

Before Reading:

- What do I know about this topic?
    - *I know that some animals have very long noses.*
    - *I know that some animals use their noses to find food.*
- What do I want to learn about this topic?
    - *I want to learn which animals have special noses.*
    - *I want to learn why special noses are helpful.*

During Reading:

- What have I learned so far?
    - *I have learned that a special nose is an adaptation.*
    - *I have learned that adaptations help living things survive.*
- I wonder why...
    - *I wonder why female proboscis monkeys like the loudest males.*
    - *I wonder why star-nosed moles can't see very well.*

After Reading:

- What did I learn about this topic?
    - *I have learned that a paddlefish uses its nose like a feeler to find food.*
    - *I have learned that a kiwi has nostrils at the end of its beak.*
- Read the book again and look for the glossary words.
    - *I see the word **survive** on page 3 and the word **mate** on page 8. The other glossary words are found on pages 22 and 23.*

NOSE NINJAS!

An **adaptation** is something that helps a living thing **survive**.

Having a special nose is one adaptation.

These animals are nose ninjas!

An elephant uses its long trunk in many ways.

Its trunk picks up food and slurps up water.

An elephant also smells and breathes through its trunk.

A paddlefish lives in rivers.

It eats tiny animals that are hard to see.

Its nose acts like a feeler to find food in the muddy water.

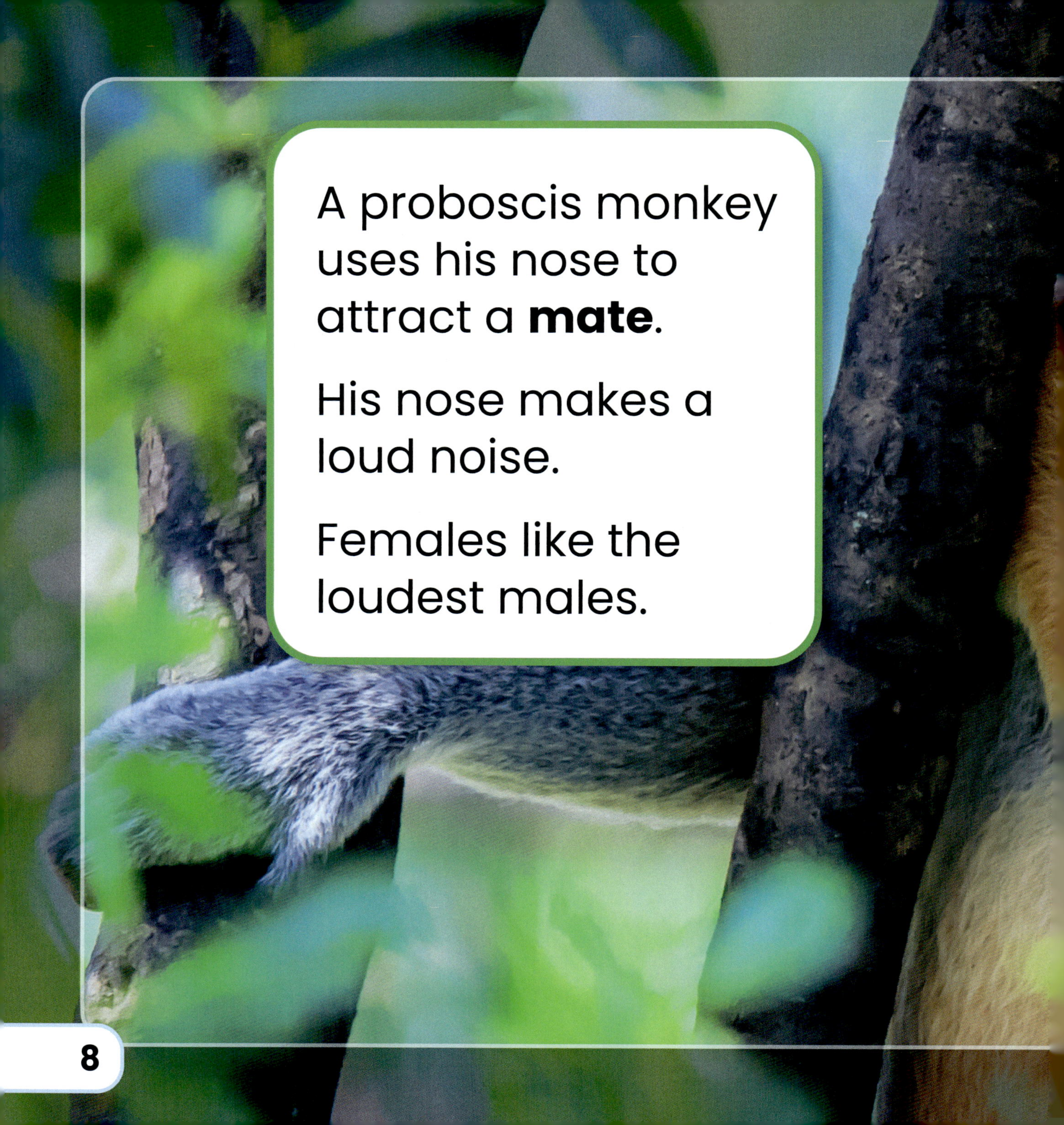

A proboscis monkey uses his nose to attract a **mate**.

His nose makes a loud noise.

Females like the loudest males.

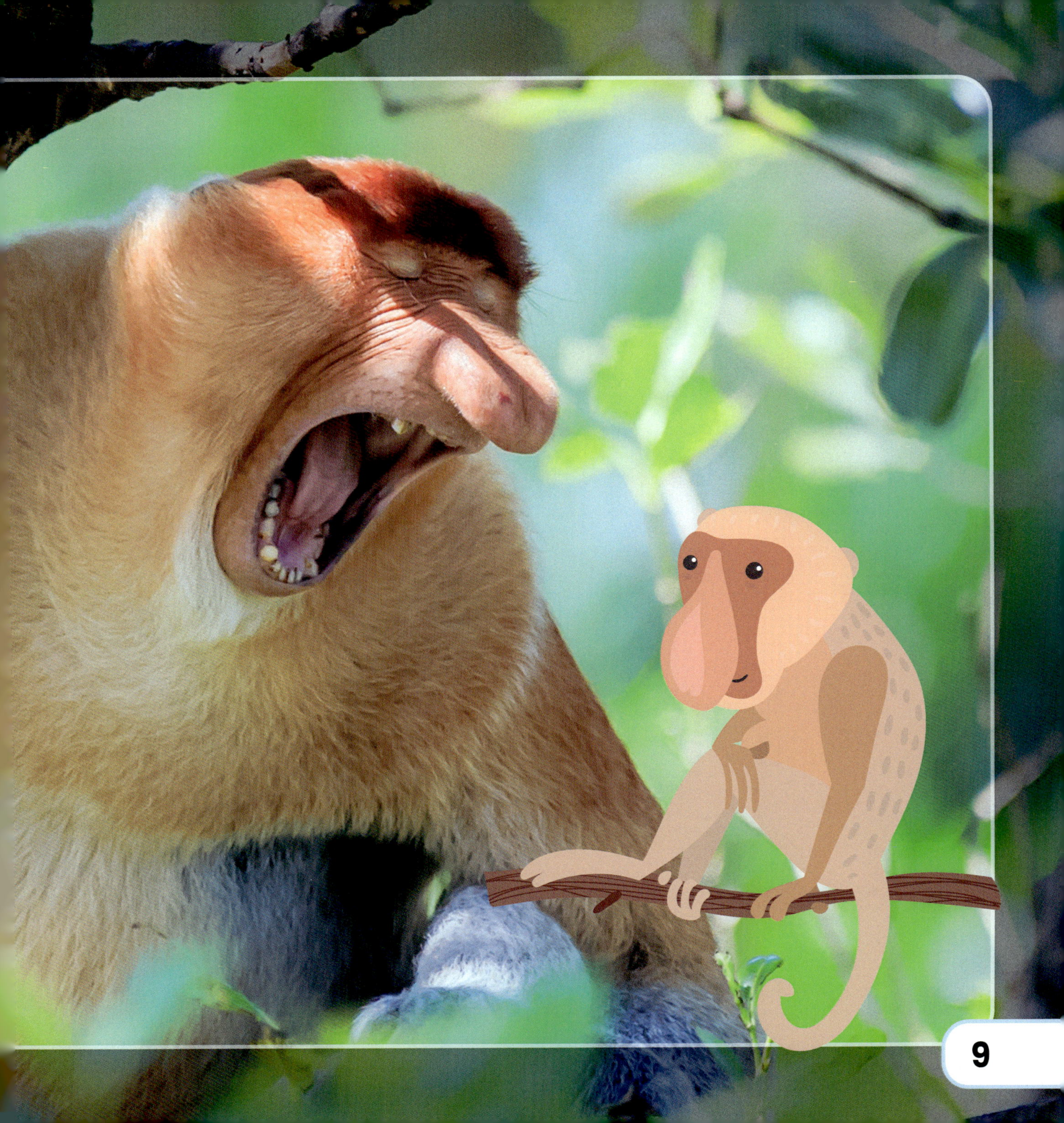

A star-nosed mole
lives underground.

It does not see well.

Its feels with its nose
to find its way.

A star-nosed mole has 22 feelers on its nose.

A saiga's nose helps it stay healthy.

Its nose keeps out dust in the dry summer.

It warms up cold air the saiga breathes in during winter.

An elephant seal uses his nose to make loud sounds.

He chases away other males.

An elephant seal grows his big nose when he's about seven years old.

An acorn weevil uses her long nose like a **drill**.

She makes a hole in an acorn.

Then she lays her eggs inside.

A kiwi has **nostrils** at the end of its beak.

It puts its beak into the **soil**.

It sniffs out worms and seeds to eat.

The kiwi is the only bird in the world with nostrils at the end of its beak.

A black bear has a big nose.

Its nose helps it smell food that is far away.

A special nose is a helpful adaptation for many living things!

Glossary

adaptation (ad-uhp-TEY-shuhn): A change in an animal or a plant that helps it live in a certain place

drill (dril): A tool with a pointed end that is used for making holes in hard materials

mate (meyt): The male or female of a pair of animals or birds

nostrils (NOS-truhlz): The two openings of the nose

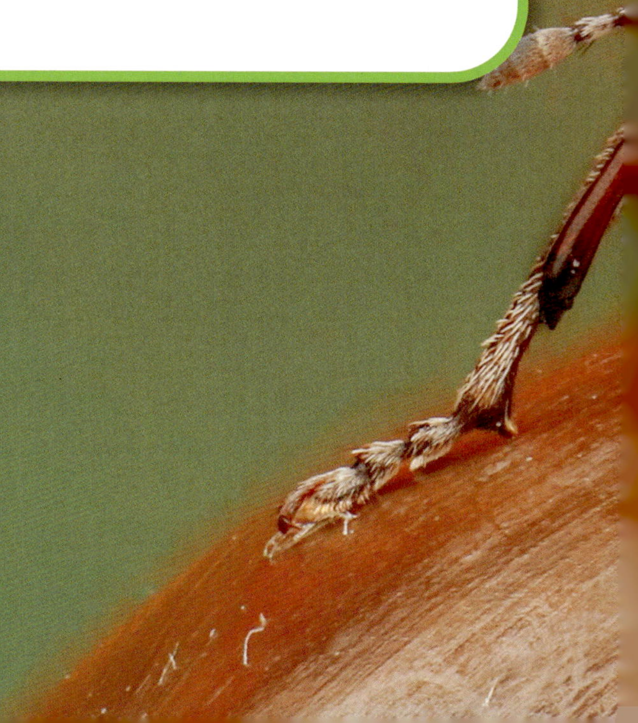

soil (soil): The top layer of earth where plants grow

survive (ser-VAHYV): To continue to live

Index

About the Author

Tracy Vonder Brink loves to learn about science and nature. She has written more than 100 nonfiction books for kids. Tracy lives in Cincinnati, Ohio, with her husband, two daughters, and two rescue dogs.

Written by: Tracy Vonder Brink
Designed by: Margaret Salter
Proofreader: Melissa Boyce
Photographs: All images from Shutterstock

Crabtree Publishing

crabtreebooks.com 800-387-7650

Printed in the U.S.A./CP2025

Published in Canada
Crabtree Publishing
616 Welland Avenue
St. Catharines, Ontario
L2M 5V6

Published in the United States
Crabtree Publishing
347 Fifth Avenue
Suite 1402-145
New York, New York, 10016

Library and Archives Canada Cataloguing in Publication
Available at Library and Archives Canada

Library of Congress Cataloging-in-Publication Data
Available at the Library of Congress

Hardcover: 978-1-0398-8112-9
Paperback: 978-1-0398-8473-1
Ebook (pdf): 978-1-0398-8232-4
Epub: 978-1-0398-8352-9
Read-Along: 978-1-0398-8557-8
Audio: 978-1-0398-8515-8